Masterworks for Violin

PAGANINI - TWO PIECES

for Violin and Piano
La Campanella - Moto Perpetuo

Edited by Endre Granat

PREFACE

Niccolò Paganini gave the premiere performance of his *Second Violin Concerto* at La Scala in Milan, 1827. The success of the performance was such that the last movement of the concerto was repeated. The subtitle of this movement is *La Campanella* (The Little Bell) because of the sound the harmonics in this work produce. Paganini, known for his pyrotechnics, uses double harmonics and left-hand pizzicato lavishly in this movement.

Moto Perpetuo is one of Paganini's most popular works. Dozens of transcriptions exist for a variety of instruments, from marimba to double bass, as well as for orchestra, where all first violins play the solo part. The 3,032 sixteenth notes in this four-minute composition require formidable skill and endurance from the performer.

Endre Granat, Editor

KEISER®

LA CAMPANELLA

Edited by
ENDRE GRANAT

NICCOLO PAGANINI
Op. 7

TWO PIECES FOR VIOLIN AND PIANO

LA CAMPANELLA

Edited by
ENDRE GRANAT

NICCOLO PAGANINI
Op. 7

Violin

Violin

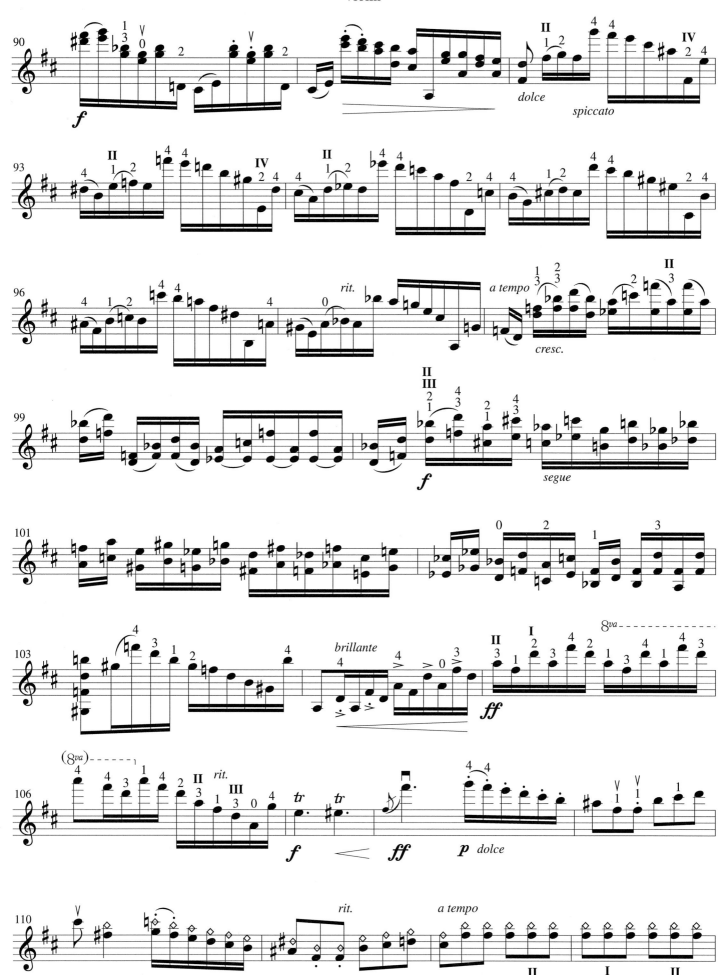

Violin

Violin

Violin

MOTO PERPETUO

Edited by
ENDRE GRANAT

NICCOLO PAGANINI
Op. 11

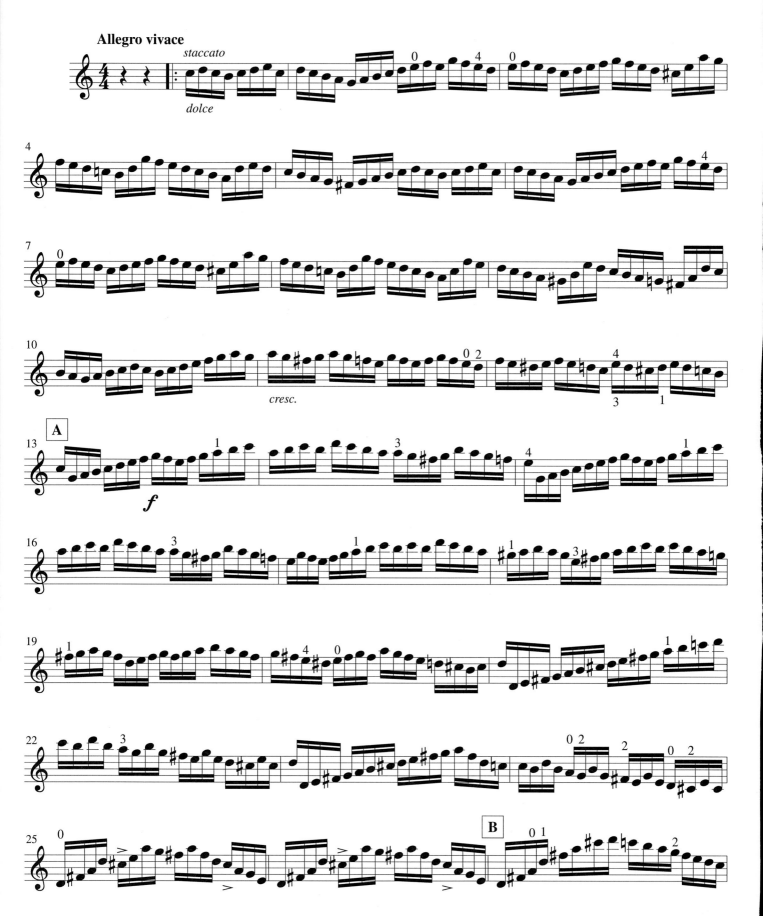

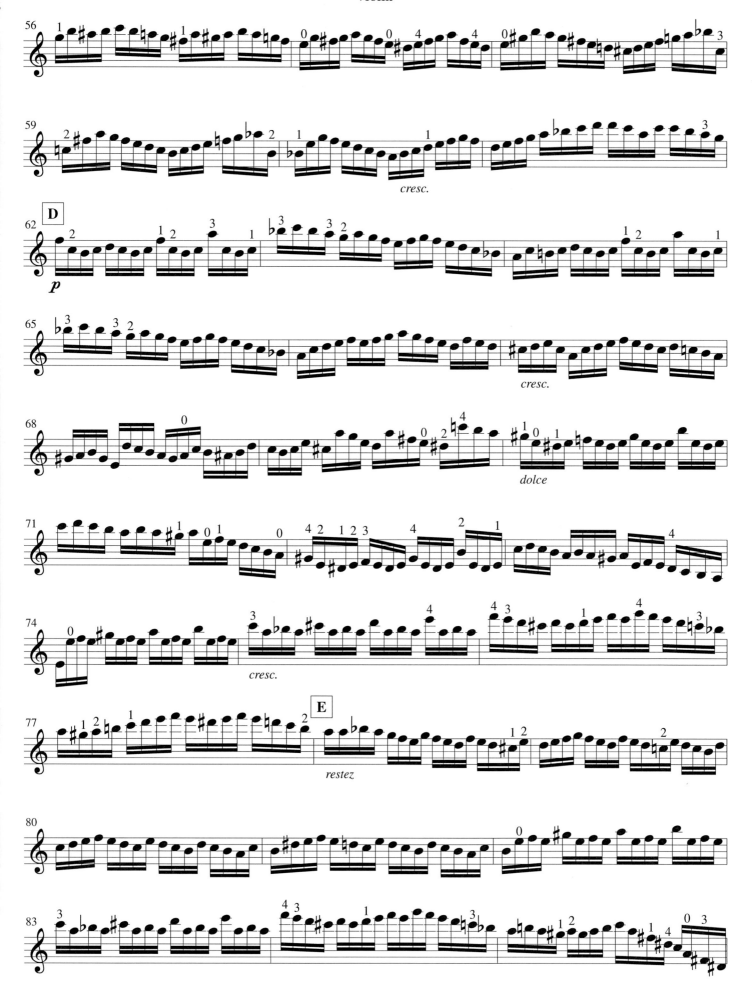

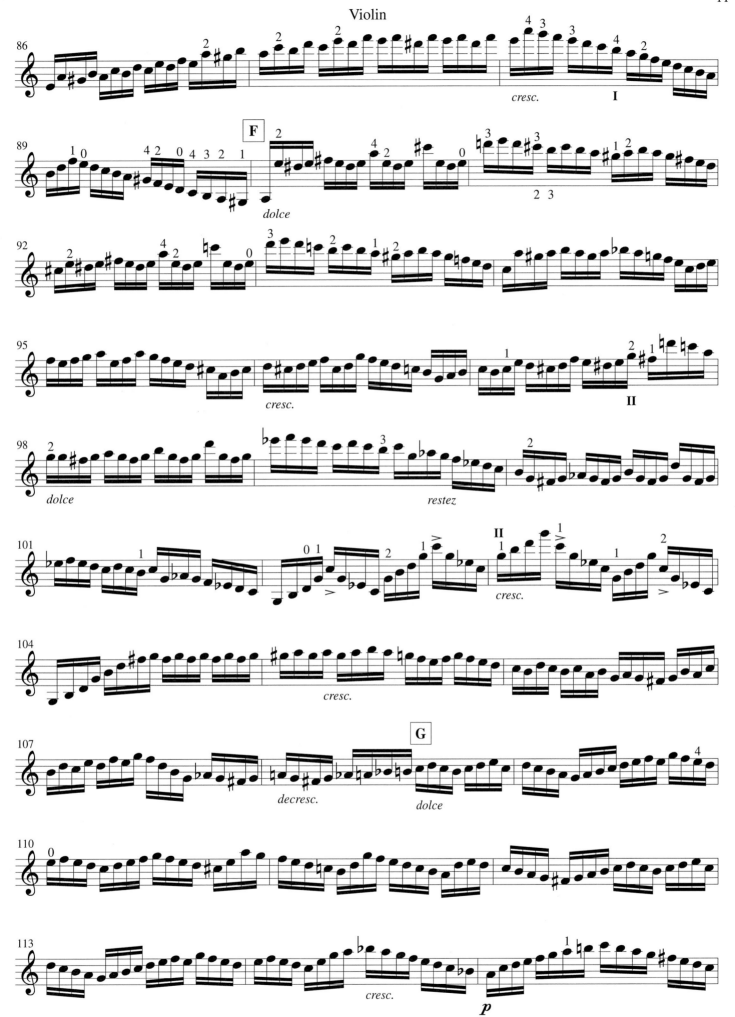

Violin

MOTO PERPETUO

Edited by
ENDRE GRANAT

NICCOLO PAGANINI
Op. 11

18